Thank you for buying my book

I love hearing your feedback and I read every single review!

Please send your comments, ideas, compliments
and anything else to me at:
VanessaLee5179@gmail.com

Other Adult Coloring books by Vanessa Lee

Color Zen Adult Coloring Book: Easy Breezy Garden Patterns

Color Zen Adult Coloring Book: Stress Relieving Forest Patterns

In this book

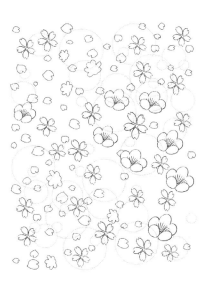

Color Zen Adult Coloring Book
"Stress Relieving Flower Patterns"

By: Vanessa Lee

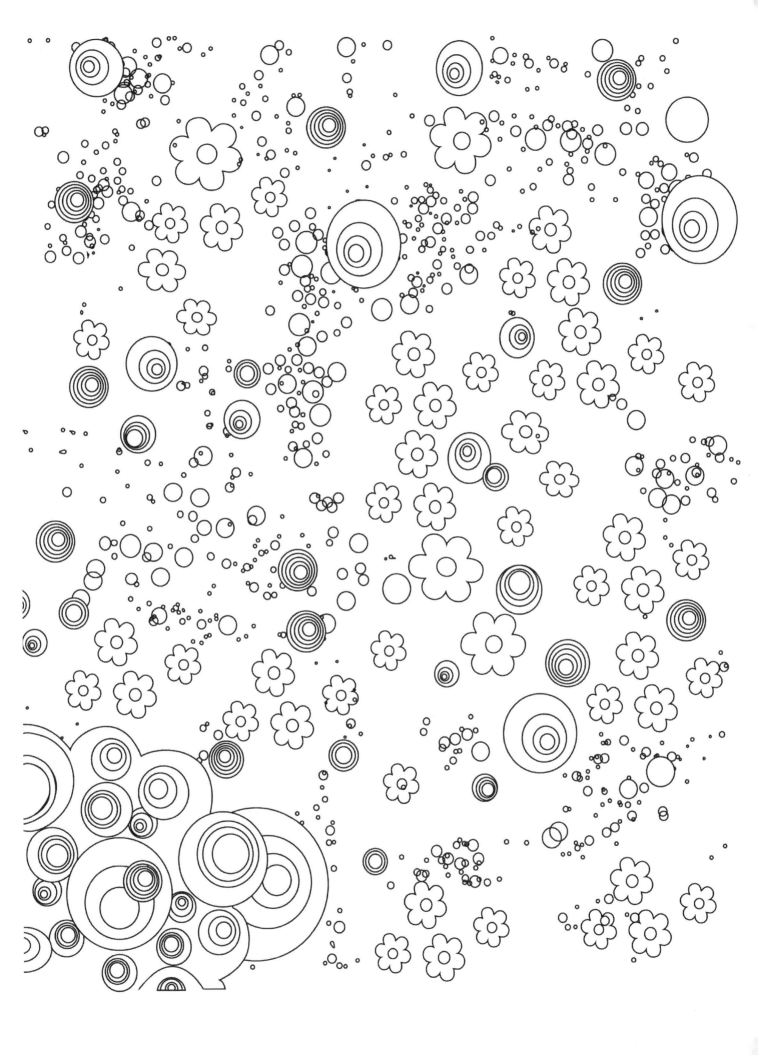

– The End –

(for now...)

28436486R00030

Made in the USA
San Bernardino, CA
29 December 2015